# Cool Hotels
## USA

# teNeues

# Imprint

Produced by fusion publishing GmbH, Stuttgart . Los Angeles    www.fusion-publishing.com

Editorial team: Martin Nicholas Kunz (Editor + Layout)
Patrice Farameh (Introduction, "What's special" texts)
Viviana Guastalla, Nathalie Grolimund, Kristin Kress (Editorial coordination)
Sabine Scholz (Text coordination), Alphagriese (Translation coordination French, English): Stéphanie Laloix (French),
Christine Grimm (US-English); Federica Bennetti, Romina Russo (Italian), Sylvia Lyschik + Sergio Ramos Ramos (Spanish)
Everbest Printing Co.Ltd - www.everbest.com, Jan Hausberg (Prepress + imaging)

Cover photo (location): courtesy The Magnolia Hotel Houston (The Magnolia Hotel Houston)

Back cover photos from top to bottom (location): Martin N. Kunz (The Setai), courtesy MGM MIRAGE (The Hotel at
Mandalay Bay), Gavin Jackson (Post Ranch Inn), Martin N. Kunz (The Standard Downtown), courtesy Dunton Hot Springs
(Dunton Hot Springs)

Photos (location): Auggie Salbosa (Hana-Maui and Honua Spa, p.62), Basil Childers (Jupiter Hotel), Cesar Rubio (Hotel Vi-
tale), courtesy Chateau Marmont (Chateau Marmont), courtesy Crescent Beverly Hills (Crescent Beverly Hills), courtesy
Dunton Hot Springs (Dunton Hot Springs), courtesy El Capitan Canyon (El Capitan Canyon), courtesy Graves 601 Hotel
(Graves 601 Hotel), courtesy Hollywood Roosevelt Hotel (Hollywood Roosevelt Hotel), courtesy Kor Hotel Group (Viceroy
Santa Monica), courtesy MGM MIRAGE (The Hotel at Mandalay Bay), courtesy The Bowery Hotel (The Bowery Hotel),
courtesy The Lowell Hotel (The Lowell Hotel), courtesy The Magnolia Hotel Houston (The Magnolia Hotel Houston),
courtesy Townhouse Miami (Townhouse Miami), courtesy Wheatleigh (Wheatleigh), courtesy W San Diego (W San Di-
ego), courtesy XV Beacon (XV Beacon), David Phelps (Hotel Ändra, Hotel Lucia, Hotel Max, Hotel Murano Tacoma), Dorit
Thies © 2007 (Miracle Manor Retreat, p.193), Emilie Elizabeth (Korakia), Gavin Jackson (The Mercer Hotel, The Mosser,
Hotel Adagio, Hotel des Arts, Post Ranch Inn, Parker Palm Springs), Holger Leue (Hana-Maui and Honua Spa, p.60, 61),
Jeffery Newbury (Hotel Vitale, p.105) John Linden photography (The Keating Hotel), Karin Kohlberg (The Lowell Hotel,
p.24, 25, 29), Lane Barden © 2007 (Miracle Manor Retreat), Michelle Galindo (The Hotel on the Beach, The Hotel), Paul
Bardagjy (Thunderbird), Tony Novak-Clifford (Hana-Maui and Honua Spa, p.63)
All other photos by Martin Nicholas Kunz

Price orientation: $ = < $200, $$ = $201 – $350, $$$ = $351 – $550, $$$$ = > $551


Published by teNeues Publishing Group

teNeues Verlag GmbH + Co. KG
Am Selder 37
47906 Kempen, Germany
Tel.: 0049-(0)2152-916-0
Fax: 0049-(0)2152-916-111
E-mail: books@teneues.de

teNeues Publishing Company
16 West 22nd Street
New York, NY 10010, USA
Tel.: 001-212-627-9090
Fax: 001-212-627-9511

teNeues Publishing UK Ltd.
P.O. Box 402
West Byfleet
KT14 7ZF, Great Britain
Tel.: 0044-1932-403509
Fax: 0044-1932-403514

teNeues France S.A.R.L.
93, rue Bannier
45000 Orléans, France
Tel.: 0033-2-38541071
Fax: 0033-2-38625340

Press department: arehn@teneues.de
Tel.: 0049-(0)2152-916-202

www.teneues.com

ISBN: 978-3-8327-9248-0

© 2008 teNeues Verlag GmbH + Co. KG, Kempen

Printed in China

Bibliographic information published by Die Deutsche Bibliothek.
Die Deutsche Bibliothek lists this publication in the Deutsche Nationalbibliografie;
detailed bibliographic data is available in the Internet at http://dnb.ddb.de.

# Contents

**Page**

# Introduction

It is just a decade ago that designer hotels were a rarity, thus overbooked and in high de-mand. These posh palaces of style—such as the ones designed by Philippe Starck—were the hottest places to sleep and dine in the United States. Due to its intense fame among savvy travelers and partygoers, a wave of boutique hotels developed by forward-thinking hoteliers such as Ian Schrager and André Balazs sprang up across the country like wildfire. As a result, this design philosophy has become the norm.

Boutique hotels today have to keep reinventing themselves in order to keep their competi-tive edge. The label as cool hotel encompasses more than just creating an extravagant stage for the hipster crowd. High-tech amenities that were once unique extras are just as important as fantastical design. Flat-screen televisions, iPod docking stations, and rainfall showers are all becoming standard comforts offered by these hip hotels.

Unique customer experience has also become a mandatory factor to being cool. Aside from its futuristic design, the *Standard Downtown* in Los Angeles offers guests an extrava-gant rooftop playground with spectacular views of skyscrapers reaching for the sky, com-plete with poolside cabanas and fire pits.

Some hotels are cool for their minimalist design to the point of being "no-frills-chic." Be-cause of the undeniable trends of going green, many consumers want simple pleasures in a high-design environment. As a consequence, design hotels are becoming more afford-able as they become more minimalist in design and in the amenities offered, such as the unique camping experience of *El Capitan Canyon* with its cedar cabins and safari tents on wooden decks.

Whether it's fine dining set in fashionable interiors or massages in a private cabana by the beach, these cool hotels are the perfect place to indulge in glitz, glamour, and guilty pleasures.

Patrice Farameh

# Einleitung

Vor noch einem Jahrzehnt waren Designerhotels rar gesät, daher stets ausgebucht und heiß begehrt. Die noblen und stilvollen Paläste – wie zum Beispiel die des Designers Philippe Starck – waren in den USA die angesagtesten Orte zum Schlafen und Speisen. Aufgrund der großen Beliebtheit bei anspruchsvollen Reisenden und Partygängern überrollte das Land eine Welle von Edelhotels, entworfen von avantgardistischen Hoteliers wie Ian Schrager und André Balazs. Diese Designphilosophie ist seither die Norm.

Heute müssen sich Edelhotels stets neu erfinden, um wettbewerbsfähig zu bleiben. Das Label „cooles Hotel" steht für mehr als nur dafür, einen extravaganten Schauplatz für angesagte Leute zu bieten. Hightech-Ausstattungen, die sonst zu den Extras zählten, sind heute genauso unverzichtbar wie ein außergewöhnliches Design. Flachbildschirme, iPod-Ladestationen und Regenduschen gehören inzwischen zum Standardangebot dieser angesagten Hotels. Cool zu sein bedeutet auch, den Kunden ein einzigartiges Erlebnis zu bieten. Neben seinem futuristischen Design bietet das *Standard Downtown* in Los Angeles seinen Gästen eine extravagante Dachlandschaft mit spektakulärer Aussicht auf Wolkenkratzer, die nach den Sternen greifen. Komplett ausgestattet mit Poolhütten und Feuerstellen.

Andere Hotels sind wiederum aufgrund ihres minimalistischen Designs mit wenig „Schnickschnack" cool. Da sich der Trend immer mehr zum Umweltbewusstsein hin entwickelt, fordern viele Kunden einfache Freuden in einer ausgefallenen Umgebung. Durch minimalistisches Design und einfachen Komfort werden Hotels immer erschwinglicher, wie zum Beispiel das *El Capitan Canyon*, das mit seinen Bungalows und Safarizelten auf Holzterrassen ein einzigartiges Campingerlebnis bietet.

Ob ein extravagantes Dinner in stilvollem Interieur oder Massagen in einer Privathütte am Strand, diese coolen Hotels sind der perfekte Ort, um sich in Glanz und Glamour den kleinen Lastern hinzugeben.

Patrice Farameh

## Introduction

Il y a seulement dix ans, les hôtels de designer étaient une rareté, si demandés qu'il était impossible d'y réserver une chambre. Aux Etats-Unis, ces temples du style, à l'instar de ceux imaginés par Philippe Starck, étaient les lieux les plus en vogue pour dormir et dîner. Leur renommée était si grande parmi les voyageurs et les fêtards les plus pointilleux, qu'une vague d'hôtels-boutique, conçus par des hôteliers perspicaces tels que Ian Schrager et André Balazs, a déferlé sur le pays. Et cette philosophie de design s'est finalement imposée. Aujourd'hui les hôtels-boutique doivent continuer à se réinventer pour conserver leur avance sur la concurrence. Le qualificatif d'hôtel cool embrasse bien plus que le simple fait de constituer une scène extravagante pour la foule branchée. Les équipements high-tech, qui étaient autrefois des « petits plus » uniques, sont aujourd'hui aussi importants que la beauté du design. Téléviseurs écran plat, stations d'accueil iPod et douches hydromassantes sont devenus les normes du confort offert par ces hôtels branchés.

Pour être cool, l'hôtel se doit aussi d'offrir une expérience unique à ses clients. Outre son design futuriste, le *Standard Downtown* à Los Angeles propose à ses clients un terrain de jeu extravagant sur le toit, avec des cabanes et des âtres au bord de la piscine, et pour couronner le tout, une vue spectaculaire sur les gratte-ciels de la ville.

Le facteur cool de certains hôtels est dû à leur design minimaliste, « chic sans ostentation ». S'inscrivant dans une incontestable tendance écologique, certains clients souhaitent profiter de plaisirs simples dans un cadre très tendance. Les hôtels deviennent donc plus abordables, au fur et à mesure que leur design se fait plus minimaliste, comme le montre l'expérience de camping unique proposée *El Capitan Canyon* avec ses cabanes en cèdre et ses tentes de safari sur des ponts en bois.

Que ce soit pour un dîner fin dans un cadre raffiné ou pour des massages dans une cabine privée sur la plage, ces hôtels cools sont le lieu idéal pour s'adonner au faste, au glamour et aux plaisirs coupables.

Patrice Farameh

## Introducción

Hace apenas diez años los hoteles de diseño eran una excepción y se encontraban saturados por la enorme demanda. En Estados Unidos, estos suntuosos palacios con estilo –como los hoteles diseñados por Philippe Starck– constituían los lugares más de moda donde dormir y cenar. Gracias a su enorme fama entre los viajeros entendidos y marchosos, una gran cantidad de hoteles boutique, creados por hoteleros innovadores como Ian Schrager y André Balazs, aparecieron a lo largo y ancho de la geografía norteamericana. Como consecuencia, esta filosofía del diseño se convirtió en un estándar.

Hoy en día, estos hoteles boutique tienen que reinventarse continuamente a fin de mantener su ventaja competitiva. El concepto de *cool hotel* va más allá de la creación de escenarios extravagantes para la gente de moda. Los aparatos y distracciones de alta tecnología, que una vez constituyeron un reclamo único, son hoy por hoy tan indispensables como un diseño extraordinario. Los televisores de pantalla plana, los puertos de conexión para el iPod y las duchas de lluvia ya son parte del menú habitual en estos hoteles a la última.

Otro factor imprescindible para merecer la etiqueta de hotel de moda es poder brindar a los clientes una experiencia única. Además de su diseño futurista, el *Standard Downtown* de Los Ángeles ofrece a sus huéspedes un extravagante patio en el tejado con pequeñas cabañas junto a una piscina, huecos en el suelo para encender hogueras y unas espectaculares vistas sobre los rascacielos que se alzan a su alrededor.

Otros hoteles apuestan por diseños minimalistas muy chic pero sin demasiadas florituras. Debido a la innegable tendencia hacia el ecologismo, muchos clientes prefieren los placeres sencillos en entornos modernos de diseño. Como consecuencia, muchos hoteles de diseño se están volviendo más asequibles gracias a un mayor minimalismo en su decoración y servicios. Un buen ejemplo de este fenómeno es *El Capitan Canyon* que, invitando a una experiencia de camping única, convence con sus cabañas de cedro y sus tiendas de campaña de safari sobre plataformas de madera.

Ya sea por las cenas exquisitas en interiores a la última o por los masajes en una cabaña privada al lado de la playa, estos hoteles de moda son el lugar idóneo para darse el capricho de una ración de lujo, glamour y pequeños placeres prohibidos.

Patrice Farameh

# Introduzione

Solamente dieci anni fa i design hotel erano ancora una rarità, motivo per cui erano sempre al completo e la loro richiesta immancabilmente elevata. Questi lussuosi templi dello stile – come gli hotel progettati da Philippe Starck – erano negli Stati Uniti i posti più accattivanti in cui dormire e mangiare. Grazie alla notevole fama di cui godevano tra esperti viaggiatori e amanti della vita mondana, questi boutique hotel progettati da albergatori all'avanguardia come Ian Schrager e André Balazs cominciarono a diffondersi a macchia d'olio in tutto il paese. È così che, nel settore alberghiero, la filosofia del design è diventata la norma.

Oggi i boutique hotel devono proporre sempre qualcosa di nuovo se vogliono riuscire a mantenersi al di sopra della concorrenza. Il loro appellativo di "cool" abbraccia molto più della semplice creazione di un ambiente stravagante per gente alla moda. Un tempo gli accessori high-tech rappresentavano l'unico vero extra, ora sono importanti tanto quanto un design fuori dal comune. In questi modernissimi hotel, televisioni a schermo piatto, docking stations per iPod e docce con getto a pioggia stanno diventano servizi standard. L'unicità del trattamento nei confronti della clientela è ormai un altro elemento d'obbligo per gli alberghi che desiderano essere "cool". Oltre al suo design futuristico, lo *Standard Downtown* di Los Angeles offre ai propri ospiti una stravagante zona svago sul tetto con spettacolari vedute dei grattacieli che si protendono verso l'alto, corredata da cabañas e piccole aree in cui accendere il fuoco a bordo piscina.

Alcuni alberghi hanno un design minimalista così cool da essere "modestamente chic". In linea con l'evidente tendenza a vivere nel rispetto per l'ambiente, oggi molti consumatori prediligono comfort semplici in luoghi d'alto design. Per questo motivo, alcuni design hotel stanno diventando più accessibili perché offrono design e servizi più essenziali, come lo straordinario *El Capitan Canyon*, con i suoi bungalow in legno di cedro e le tende stile safari issate su terrazze di legno.

Che si scelga una sontuosa cena servita in un ambiente alla moda o un massaggio in una cabaña privata lungo la spiaggia, questi hotel "cool" sono il posto ideale in cui abbandonarsi allo sfarzo, al glamour e ai peccati del piacere.

Patrice Farameh

# The Mercer Hotel

147 Mercer Street
SoHo
New York City, NY 10012
New York
Phone: +1 212 966 6060
Fax: +1 212 965 3838
www.mercerhotel.com

**Price category:** $$$$
**Rooms:** 75 rooms
**Facilities:** The Mercer Kitchen restaurant, bar, 24 h fitness center
**Services:** Lobby food, library, limousine service
**Located:** Mercer Street between West Houston Street and Prince Street
**Public transportation:** N, R, W at Prince Street; 6 at Spring Street; B, D, F, V at Broadway-Lafayette Street
**Map:** No. 1
**Style:** Contemporary design
**What's special:** Loft-style living with fireplaces, kitchens, and two-person bathtubs, health club offers private trainers and in-room beauty treatments, 24 h restaurant, room service, personalized service such as packing/unpacking, concierge serves as the guest's private secretary.

# Night Hotel

132 West 45th Street
Theatre District
New York City, NY 10036
New York
Phone: +1 212 835 9600
Fax: +1 212 835 9610
www.nighthotelny.com

**Price category:** $$$
**Rooms:** 72 rooms, 2 penthouse suites
**Facilities:** Bar, lounge, in-room Bose CD wave system
with iPod connectivity feature, 37-inch plasma-screen TV
**Services:** Continental breakfast, concierge, room service,
daily turn down services, and personal shopper service
**Located:** Between 6th and 7th Avenues
**Public transportation:** B, D, F, V at 47th-50th Streets-
Rockefeller Center
**Map:** No. 2
**Style:** Modern gothic
**What's special:** Stylish boutique hotel with wicked Go-
tham feel, at check-in each guest receives custom-made
personal business cards and gothic "N" non-permanent
tattoos, special access to the Chopra Center and Spa, sur-
real courtyard designed out of mirrors and grated pebbles.

# The Bowery Hotel

335 Bowery Street
NoHo
New York City, NY 10003
New York
Phone: +1 212 505 9100
Fax: +1 212 505 9700
www.theboweryhotel.com

**Price category:** $$$
**Rooms:** 135 rooms
**Facilities:** Restaurant Gemma, cocktail lounges, red-brick terraces, event space on 2nd floor
**Services:** Flat-screen TV, iPod-powered stereo, DVD player and free WiFi
**Located:** Between East 3rd Street and East 2nd Street
**Public transportation:** 6 at Bleecker Street; F, V at Lower East Side-Second Ave.; B, D, F, V at Broadway-Lafayette St.
**Map:** No. 3
**Style:** Classic old European design
**What's special:** Orchestra of different design elements from British traditional charm to Moroccan chic, Oriental rugs and hanging candelabras in intimate lobby, rooms have hardwood floors and floor-to-ceiling windows with spectacular city views of New York.

# The Lowell Hotel

28 East 63rd Street
Upper East Side
New York City, NY 10065
New York
Phone: +1 212 838 1400
Fax: +1 212 319 4230
www.lowellhotel.com

**Price category:** $$$$
**Rooms:** 47 individually decorated suites, 25 deluxe rooms
**Facilities:** Restaurant, fitness, Fiji water, fireplaces
**Services:** Multilingual staff
**Located:** East 63rd Street between Madison Avenue and Park Avenue
**Public transportation:** N, R, W at Lexington Avenue-59th Street; 4, 5, 6 at 59th Street; F at Lexington Avenue-63rd Street
**Map:** No. 4
**Style:** Contemporary design
**What's special:** First-class cuisine served on hand-painted Washington Pickard china, intimate hotel with aristocratic Old World charm in the heart of Manhattan, old-fashioned yet elegant lobby, some guestrooms have fireplace and terraces, baths have full size Bvlgari products.

# Wheatleigh

Hawthorne Road
Lenox, MA 01240
Massachusetts
Phone: +1 413 637 0610
Fax: +1 413 637 4507
www.wheatleigh.com

**Price category:** $$$$
**Rooms:** 19 rooms
**Facilities:** Restaurant, swimming pool, fitness center, spa, tennis, shops, business/meeting rooms
**Services:** High-speed Internet, room service, laundry, valet, concierge and child care services
**Located:** Close to unique galleries, shops, and museums
**Map:** No. 5
**Style:** Contemporary design combining museum quality art with custom designed furniture
**What's special:** Built in 1893 on 22 beautifully landscaped acres, grand 19th century Renaissance palazzo with 19 exquisite suites, offers in-room massages, private museum tours, traditional high tea service, extraordinary cuisine, personalized service.

# XV Beacon

15 Beacon Street
Boston, MA 02108
Massachusetts
Phone: +1 617 670 1500
US Toll Free: 877 982 3226
Fax: +1 617 670 2525
www.xvbeacon.com

**Price category:** $$$
**Rooms:** 60 rooms
**Facilities:** Mooo Restaurant, The Wine Cellar, private
dining rooms, exercise room, entertainment systems
and private bars in all rooms
**Services:** High-speed Internet, 27-inch TV in room, 24 h
valet laundry, overnight shoe shine, valet parking, eve-
ning turn down, in-room massages, 24 h concierge
**Located:** In historic Beacon Hill
**Public transportation:** Subway nearby
**Map:** No. 6
**Style:** Cosmopolitan, eclectic
**What's special:** In a 1903 beaux arts landmark building
with an eclectic mix of Jeffersonian styling and modern
technology blend the old and the new, rooms feature
gas fireplaces and rainforest shower heads.

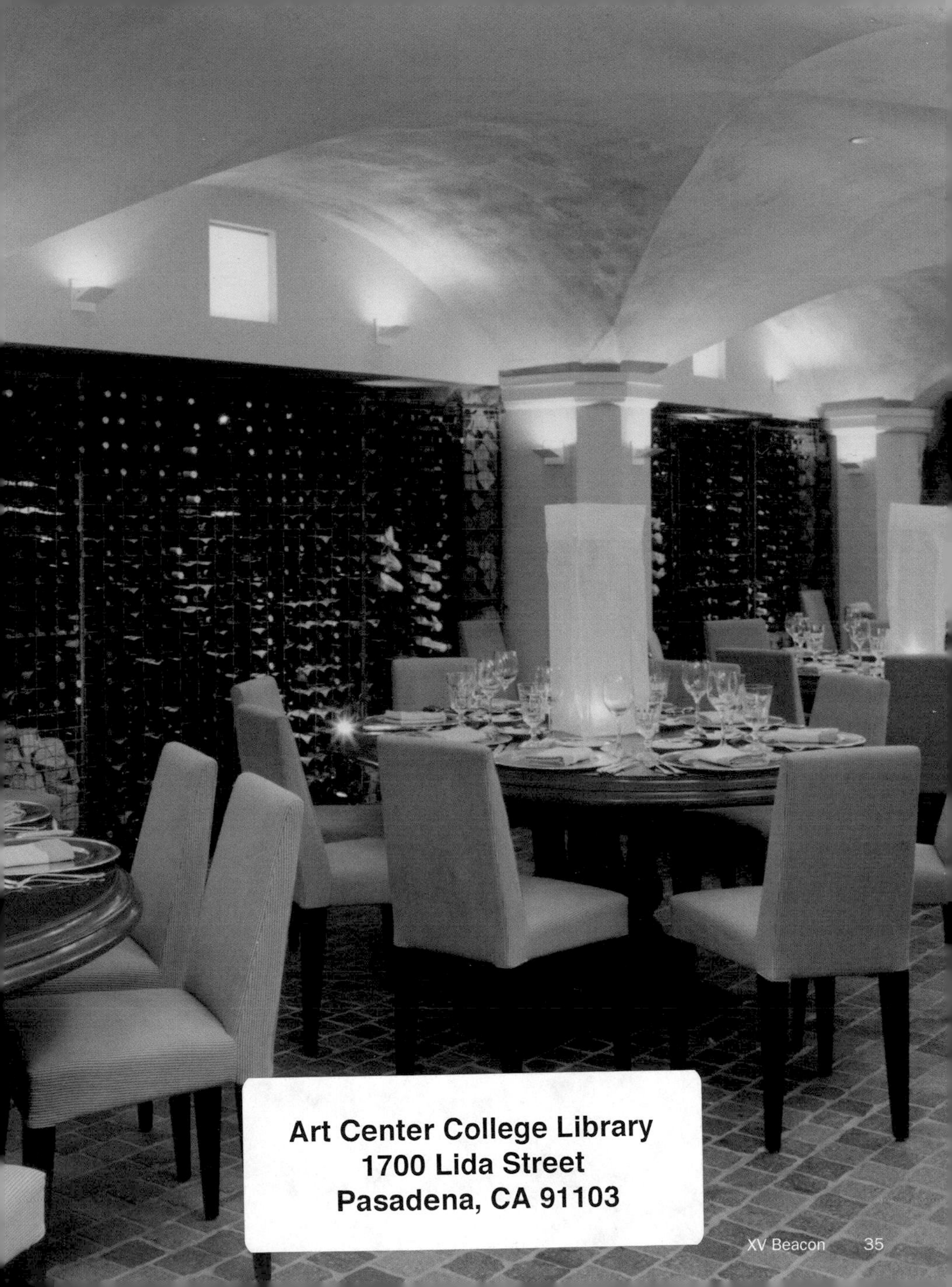

# The Hotel

801 Collins Avenue
Miami Beach, FL 33139
Florida
Phone: +1 305 531 2222
Fax: +1 305 531 3232
www.thehotelofsouthbeach.com

**Price category:** $$$
**Rooms:** 52 rooms
**Facilities:** Spire Bar & Lounge, Wish Restaurant and Bar, fitness studio, boutique group and meeting facilities
**Services:** Concierge, wireless Internet, TV, stereo and cable, minibar, maid service, valet and massage services are available in rooms and the pool deck
**Located:** Located in the heart of the Art Deco District
**Map:** No. 7
**Style:** High style, luxurious
**What's special:** Historic Art Deco hotel with ultra-luxurious rooms with rainfall showers, rooftop pool deck, Spire Bar & Lounge is a South Beach hotspot with views over the city and sea, complimentary beach towels, chairs and umbrellas.

# Casa Casuarina

1116 Ocean Drive
Miami Beach, FL 33139
Florida
Phone: +1 305 672 6604
Fax: +1 305 672 5930
www.casacasuarina.com

**Price category:** $$
**Rooms:** 10 luxury suites
**Facilities:** The Club Bar, restaurant, spa and lounge
**Services:** 24 h concierge, luxury car rental, limousine service, specialized spa services
**Located:** In the heart of Miami Beach
**Map:** No. 8
**Style:** Unique themed décor
**What's special:** The former Versace owned residence with ten suites, private invitation-only membership club for select few, now a luxury boutique hotel and event venue, thousand mosaic swimming pool, rooftop observatory for stargazing, cigar lounge, orchid-filled garden, luxury beach cabanas, boutique spa, available for private parties, weddings, corporate and social events.

# The Setai

2001 Collins Avenue
Miami Beach, FL 33139
Florida
Phone: +1 305 520 6000
US Toll Free: 888 625 7500
Fax: +1 305 520 6600
www.setai.com

**Price category:** $$$$
**Rooms:** 125 rooms
**Facilities:** Spa, three pools, hot tub, fitness center, courtyard, Asian influenced boutique, a 90-ft-long poolside bar, restaurant, grill
**Services:** Room service, 24 h concierge, kids services/ babysitting, Internet access, pets OK, laundry, valet
**Located:** Beach front
**Map:** No. 9
**Style:** A place that embraces you in its serenity
**What's special:** Elegant hotel is also luxury residential tower on popular South Beach, contemporary Zen feel with ultra-modern minimalist design with Asian art, rooms have spacious granite baths and rainfall showers, pools have areas with different water temperature.

# Townhouse Miami

150 20th Street
Miami Beach, FL 33139
Florida
Phone: +1 305 534 3800
Fax: +1 305 534 3811
www.townhousehotel.com

**Price category:** $$
**Rooms:** 69 rooms
**Facilities:** The Bond Street Lounge, rainshowers and private jacuzzis in suites
**Services:** Flat screen TVs, Internet, concierge, valet, complimentary Parisian Breakfast
**Located:** On the north edge of South Beach, the Townhouse Miami is a half-block from the beach
**Map:** No. 10
**Style:** Blend of modern design and old-fashioned comfort
**What's special:** Outdoor rooftop terrace have king-size waterbeds shaded under huge umbrellas during the day and transforms into one of South Beach's hottest social scenes in the evening, front-desk gift shop offers everything from Bacardi to "Hangover from Hell" eye masks.

# Hana-Maui and Honua Spa

Hana, HA 96713
Hawaii
Phone: +1 808 248 8211
US Toll Free: 800 321 4262
Fax: +1 808 248 7202
www.hotelhanamaui.com

**Price category:** $$$$
**Rooms:** 70 luxury rooms
**Facilities:** Restaurant, lounge bar, two swimming pools, jacuzzi, steam room, watsu pool, sport facilities, boogie boards, conference facilities, shops
**Services:** Horseback riding, bikes, Hawaiian cultural activities, custom-blend coffee, herbal teas, Internet
**Located:** Approx. 3 miles from Hana Airport
**Map:** No. 11
**Style:** Enchanting Hawaiian inspiration
**What's special:** Luxury resort sits on 67 acres of landscaped gardens with two pools, individual duplex cottages have comfy feather beds, massive soaking bathtubs, and floor-to-ceiling sliding doors, award-winning full service spa and fitness room.

# Graves 601 Hotel

601 1st Avenue North
Minneapolis, MN 55403
Minnesota
Phone: +1 612 677 1100
US Toll Free: 866 523 1100
www.graves601hotel.com

**Price category:** $$
**Rooms:** 255 rooms
**Facilities:** Restaurant and lounge, Infiniti Room, Health Club and spa, tennis court, meeting rooms, family room
**Services:** 24 h room service, minibar, laundry service, Stereo/Hi-Fi/CD player, high-speed Internet, 42-inch plasma screen TV
**Located:** In the heart of downtown Minneapolis, across the street from Target Center, one block from IDS Tower
**Public transportation:** Shuttle to Airport
**Map:** No. 12
**Style:** High technology, high fashion
**What's special:** High-tech fashionable hotel has a skyway connected to shopping districts, rooms have floor-to-ceiling etched glass partitions, bathrooms feature freestanding showers with rainfall effect.

# Thunderbird

601 West San Antonio
Marfa TX, 79843
Texas
Phone: +1 432 729 1984
Fax: +1 432 729 1989
www.thunderbirdmarfa.com

**Price category:** $
**Rooms:** 24 rooms
**Facilities:** Lounge, boutique, swimming pool, patio lounge
**Services:** Wireless high-speed Internet, vintage typewriter, vintage Stack-O-Matic record players and vinyl library, bike rentals
**Located:** 200 miles from El Paso and Midland
**Map:** No. 13
**Style:** Minimalist comfort
**What's special:** Small boutique hotel built in 1959 on the northeastern edge of the Chihuahuan Desert set over a mile high, poolside lounge set in an exotic garden of indigenous plants, impressive views of dramatic mountainous desert.

# The Magnolia Hotel Houston

1100 Texas Avenue
Houston, TX 77002
Texas
Phone: +1 713 221 00 11
US Toll Free: 888 915 1110
www.magnoliahotelhouston.com

**Price category:** $$
**Rooms:** 314 rooms, Ross Sterling Presidential Suite
**Facilities:** Magnolia Club, library, 24 h fitness center, rooftop pool and jacuzzi, billiards room, grand ballroom
**Services:** Complimentary hot American breakfast buffet, late-night fresh-baked cookies and milk, downtown car service
**Located:** Downtown Houston, close to Minute Maid Park
**Map:** No. 14
**Style:** Contemporary style in a renovated, historic building
**What's special:** Housed in the historic Post Dispatch Building, the 22-story hotel was hailed as one of the most impressive office buildings in the state. The gorgeous 1,200-square feet Ross Sterling Presidential Suite features a black and white tile floor. The rooftop pool and patio boasts amazing views of downtown.

# Dunton Hot Springs

52068 County Road 38
Dolores, CO 81323
Colorado
Phone: +1 970 882 4800
Fax: +1 970 882 7474
www.duntonhotsprings.com

**Price category:** $$
**Rooms:** 12 guest cabins
**Facilities:** Mineral rich hot springs, saloon, dance hall, library, gym, chapel and screening room
**Services:** Yoga, horseback riding, high-speed Internet, fireplaces, room service, satellite TV, newspaper, shuttle service available
**Located:** In Southwestern Colorado
**Map:** No. 15
**Style:** Natural design
**What's special:** Hotel set in a romantic ghost town surrounded by the Alpine Valley, authentic saloon serving high-quality meals, hand-hewn log cabins with luxurious furnishings, natural hot springs with first rate spa, nature hiking trails.

# Sanctuary on Camelback Mountain

5700 East McDonald Drive
Paradise Valley, AZ 85253
Arizona
Phone: +1 480 948 2100
US Toll Free: 800 245 2051
Fax: +1 480 483 3386
www.SanctuaryAZ.com

**Price category:** $$$$
**Rooms:** 98 casitas and 7 private homes
**Facilities:** Swimming pool, elements restaurant, jade bar, edge bar, spa, meeting and banquet facilities
**Services:** 24 h room service, nightly candlelight turn-down service with relaxing signature lavender linen spray
**Located:** 15 min to Phoenix International Airport
**Map:** No. 16
**Style:** Contemporary elegance
**What's special:** Luxury boutique hideaway with dramatic mountain and spa casitas with spectacular views of Paradise Valley, Sanctuary Spa has 14 indoor/outdoor treatment rooms, relaxing meditation garden, five tennis courts, extensive wine list, 25-yard lap pool, Arizona's largest infinity-edge pool.

# The Hotel at Mandalay Bay

3950 Las Vegas Boulevard South
Las Vegas, NV 89119
Nevada
Phone: +1 877 632 7000
US Toll Free: 877 632 7800
Fax: +1 702 632 7108
www.thehotelatmandalaybay.com

**Price category:** $
**Rooms:** 1,117 room suites
**Facilities:** Spa, gym, Mix Lounge, billiards lounge, lobby bar, coffee bar, cafe
**Services:** Plasma TVs, high-speed Internet, and minibar await the guests in their room
**Located:** On the southern end of the Las Vegas Strip
**Map:** No. 17
**Style:** Modern Sofistication
**What's special:** Luxury hotel in the heart of Las Vegas, stylish lobby is casino-free, spacious suites are focused on minimalist design in tranquil tones of gray, world-class mega-spa Bathhouse, celebrated chef Alain Ducasse's only Las Vegas dining temple Mix located on the 52nd floor.

# The Mosser

54 Fourth Street
San Francisco, CA 94103
California
Phone: +1 415 986 4400
US Toll Free: 800 227 3804
Fax: +1 415 495 7653
www.themosser.com

**Price category:** $$
**Rooms:** 166 rooms
**Facilities:** Annabelle's Bar and Bistro, Studio Paradiso, fitness center
**Services:** Valet parking and laundry service available, CD player, Internet access, bathrobes, ceiling fan
**Located:** Within four blocks of Union Square and even closer to Sony Metreon and Moscone Center
**Public transportation:** Metro, Powell Street
**Map:** No. 18
**Style:** Hip boutique
**What's special:** Modern hotel has its own recording studio, perfect for the stylish traveler on a budget, historic property is over 100 years old, recently renovated with modern interior design combined with its Victorian architecture.

# Hotel Adagio

550 Geary Street
San Francisco, CA 94102
California
Phone: +1 415 775 5000
Fax: : +1 415 775 9388
www.jdvhotels.com

**Price category:** $
**Rooms:** 171 Rooms
**Facilities:** Cortez Restaurant, bar, lounge, fitness center, business center, meeting room and conference rooms
**Services:** In-room dining, morning town car service M-F 7am-9am to Financial District, Internet, laundry, valet
**Located:** In the heart of San Francisco's theater district
**Public transportation:** Cable Car
**Map:** No. 19
**Style:** Fresh contemporary
**What's special:** Spanish colonial hotel combined with clean style of contemporary design, large Executive Level guestrooms come with modern amenities such as stereos with iPod ports and have dramatic San Francisco city views from the top floors, award-winning restaurant Cortez.

447 Bush Street
San Francisco, CA 94108
California
Phone: +1 415 956 3232
US Toll Free: 800 956 4322
Fax: +1 415 956 0399
www.sfhoteldesarts.com

**Price category:** $
**Rooms:** 51 rooms
**Facilities:** Restaurant, parking garage available nearby (surcharge)
**Services:** Complimentary continental breakfast, wireless Internet, 24 h concierge, airport transport
**Located:** Downtown San Francisco, a half-block from main entrance to Chinatown, close to financial district
**Public transportation:** Metro, Cable Car
**Map:** No. 20
**Style:** Rooms painted by emerging artists
**What's special:** Luxury hotel has its own gallery, each of the guest rooms are painted with themes from emerging artists from around the world, some artist-designed rooms have art installations or cutting-edge graffiti works of art.

# Hotel Vitale

8 Mission Street
San Francisco, CA 94105
California
Phone: +1 415 278 3700
US Toll Free: 888 890 8688
Fax: +1 415 278 3750
www.hotelvitale.com

**Price category:** $$$
**Rooms:** 199 rooms
**Facilities:** Americano restaurant, bar with outdoor patio, fitness room, business center
**Services:** Yoga and stretching classes, penthouse-level private soaking tubs in secret garden, spa services, high-speed Internet access and WiFi in guestrooms
**Located:** Across the street from the revitalized Embarcadero waterfront in San Francisco
**Public transportation:** BART & MUNI
**Map:** No. 21
**Style:** Post-hip, urban, revitalizing
**What's special:** Modern interior design hotel as urban oasis overlooking stunning views of landmark vistas and the bay, on-site spa with outdoor rooftop soaking bathtubs, panoramic circular suites.

# Post Ranch Inn

Highway 1
Big Sur, CA 93920
California
Phone: +1 831 667 2200
US Toll Free: 800 527 2200
Fax: +1 831 667 2512
www.postranchinn.com

**Price category:** $$$$
**Rooms:** 40 rooms, Post House with 3 bedrooms, South Coast House with 2 bedrooms
**Facilities:** Restaurant, wine cellar, spa
**Services:** Free parking, Internet access
**Located:** Nestled on the cliffs of Big Sur, 1 h driving from Monterey airport, 2.5 h from San Francisco
**Map:** No. 22
**Style:** Modern country chic
**What's special:** Extravagant modern lodge has angular architecture with rusted steel, perched 365 meters above the sea on a cliff with breathtaking views of the ocean, tree-house villas have a cozy fireplace and private deck, in-room spa treatments from dawn until midnight.

# El Capitan Canyon

11560 Calle Real
Santa Barbara, CA 93117
California
Phone: +1 805 685 3887
US Toll Free: 866 352 2729
Fax: +1 805 968 6772
www.elcapitancanyon.com

**Price category:** $$
**Rooms:** 26 safari tents and 108 cedar cabins
**Facilities:** Meeting/banquet facilities, spa, retail store, café, pool, ropes course
**Services:** Concierge, free parking, shuttle
**Located:** 20 miles north of downtown Santa Barbara
**Map:** No. 23
**Style:** Contemporary Rustic
**What's special:** Resort for those who want to connect with nature through a unique lodging experience. Fully furnished safari tents and cedar cabins on 300 acres have access to hiking and biking trails and are walking distance from the beach.

# Viceroy Santa Monica

1819 Ocean Avenue
Santa Monica, CA 90401
California
Phone: +1 310 260 7500
Fax: +1 310 260 7515
www.viceroysantamonica.com

**Price category:** $$$
**Rooms:** 162 guestrooms and suites
**Facilities:** Restaurant, bar, cabanas, two outdoor pools, fitness center, library, valet parking for surcharge
**Services:** Over-sized showers, wireless/wired high-speed Internet, 27-inch flat screen TV, 24 h room service, choice of daily newspaper, laundry and dry cleaning
**Located:** Ocean Avenue and Pico Boulevard in Los Angeles
**Map:** No. 24
**Style:** English colonial, cosmopolitan spirit
**What's special:** Modern 8-story seaside refuge combines stylish sophistication with contemporary chic, impressive outdoor courtyard dining area with dining options in private cabanas, most guestrooms have French balconies, sexy mirrored walls and spectacular ocean views.

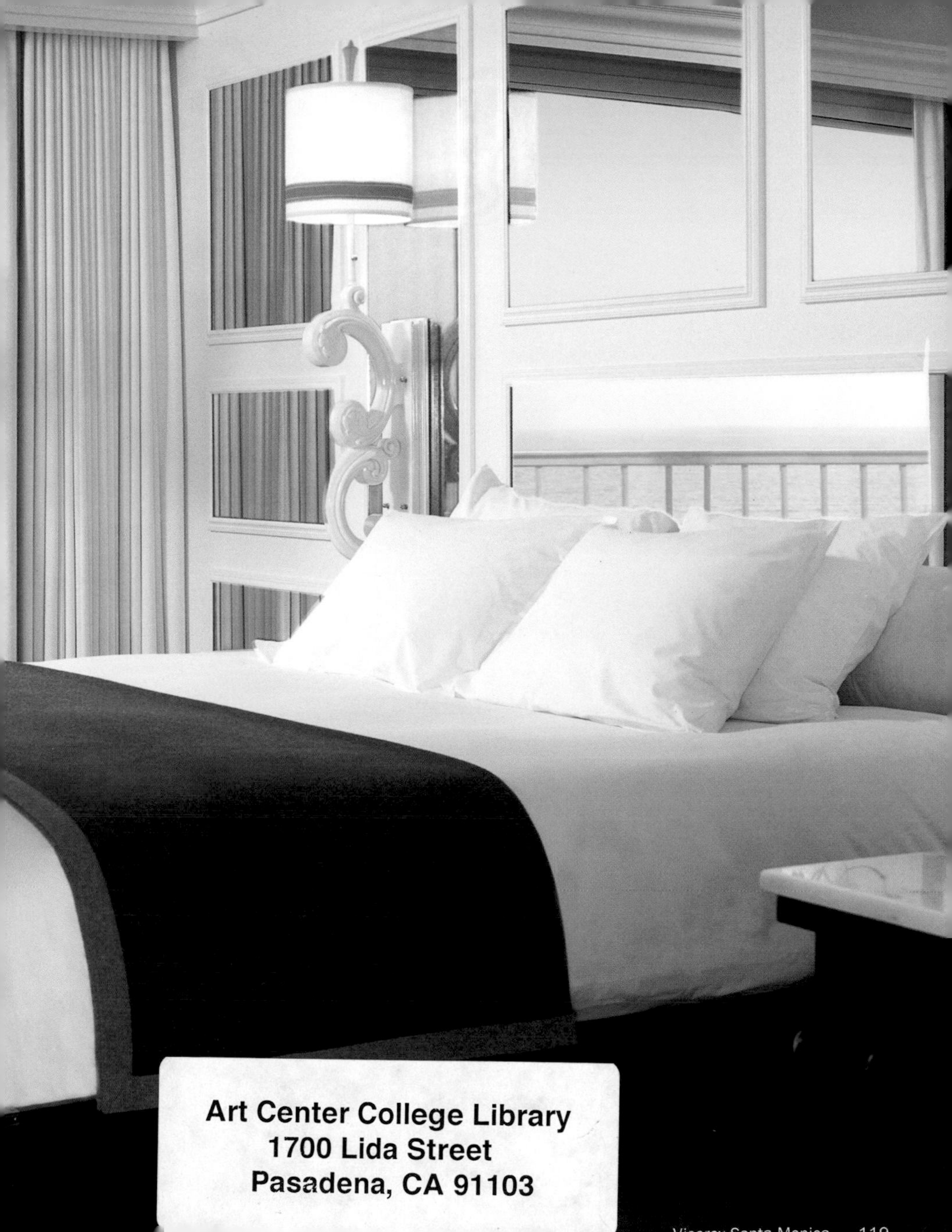

# Shutters The Hotel on the Beach

1 Pico Boulevard
Santa Monica, CA 90405
California
Phone: +1 310 458 0030
US Toll Free: 800 334 9000
Fax: +1 310 458 4589
www.shuttersonthebeach.com

**Price category:** $$$$
**Rooms:** 186 guest rooms and 12 suites
**Facilities:** One Pico Restaurant, Coast Beach Café and Bar, spa, pool, jacuzzi, fitness center, health club
**Services:** 24 h room service, fireplace in rooms, minibar, Internet access, whirlpool, DVD and newspaper
**Located:** Sits perfectly on the sand of Santa Monica Bay
**Public transportation:** Big Blue Bus, Santa Monica Bus
**Map:** No. 25
**Style:** Traditional architecture of America's historic beach resorts during the 1920s and 1930s
**What's special:** Beachfront hotel where each guest room is designed like a private beach cottage with balconies with ocean views, expansive spa menu at One, pool deck and ocean terrace with two fireplaces and full service, two seaside restaurants.

# Crescent Beverly Hills

403 North Crescent Drive
Beverly Hills, CA 90210
California
Phone: +1 310 247 0505
Fax: +1 310 247 9053
www.crescentbh.com

**Price category:** $$
**Rooms:** 35 rooms
**Facilities:** Two landscaped and secluded patios
**Services:** First-class amenities such as Aveda bath products, down comforters, robes and slippers, in-room wireless Internet access, dry cleaning, overnight parking, 24 h front desk and concierge
**Located:** On the quiet corner of Beverly Hills' Golden Triangle, two blocks from Rodeo Drive
**Public transportation:** Metro, Santa Monica/Crescent-SW
**Map:** No. 26
**Style:** Contemporary sleek, cozy boutique hotel
**What's special:** Hotel built in 1926 for silent film stars located in the heart of Beverly Hills, completely renovated with Art Deco exteriors, interiors designed with relaxing retro-modern feel, chic lounge and restaurant.

# Hollywood Roosevelt Hotel

7000 Hollywood Boulevard
Los Angeles, CA 90028
California
Phone: +1 323 466 7000
Fax: +1 323 462 8056
www.thompsonhotels.com

**Price category:** $$$
**Rooms:** 300 rooms, 60 suites, 1 penthouse
**Facilities:** Poolside cabanas, Gable & Lombard Penthouse, Dakota Restaurant, Teddy's, library bar, poolside bar, swimming pool
**Services:** WiFi, room service, concierge, laundry service, parking (fee), no-smoking rooms, minibar
**Located:** In the heart of Hollywood
**Public transportation:** Hollywood/Highland METRO
**Map:** No. 27
**Style:** Modern design
**What's special:** Birthplace of the Academy Awards, playground for celebrities and renowned figures since 1927, acclaimed designer Dodd Mitchell headed renovations for a more youthful, hip appearance.

# Chateau Marmont

8221 Sunset Boulevard
Los Angeles, CA 90046
California
Phone: +1 323 656 1010
Fax: +1 323 655 5311
www.chateaumarmont.com

**Price category:** $$$$
**Rooms:** 63 rooms
**Facilities:** Heated outdoor pool, fitness room, tennis courts, golf course
**Services:** Intimate dining room, valet parking, iPod docking stations, 24 h concierge and room service
**Located:** Off Sunset Boulevard in Hollywood
**Map:** No. 28
**Style:** Modeled after an infamous royal residence in France's Loire Valley
**What's special:** Most legendary castle in Hollywood offers best views of Los Angeles and caters to movie stars, famous hotel has made countless tabloid headlines, some bungalows have fully-stocked kitchens, dining rooms and balconies or private terraces.

# Farmer's Daughter

115 South Fairfax Avenue
Los Angeles, CA 90036
California
Phone: +1 323 937 3930
Fax: +1 323 932 1608
www.farmersdaughterhotel.com

**Price category:** $
**Rooms:** 66 rooms
**Facilities:** Tart Restaurant, bar, pool, business center
**Services:** Internet access, room service, concierge services, daily laundry and dry cleaning
**Located:** Within walking distance from the Farmers Market, the Grove, theaters, restaurants and shopping, Fairfax Village, CBS Studios, L.A. County Museum of Art
**Map:** No. 29
**Style:** Comfy modern
**What's special:** Unique urban oasis combined with countryside laid back charm, all 66 guest rooms have comfortable traditional furnishings and style mixed with modern design, "his and hers" rooms feature denim bedspreads, rocking chairs, and hardwood-inspired floors

# Custom Hotel

8639 Lincoln Boulevard
Los Angeles, CA 90045
California
Phone: +1 310 645 0400
Fax: +1 310 645 0700
www.customhotel.com

**Price category:** $
**Rooms:** 250 guest rooms and suites
**Facilities:** Restaurant Bistrotek, bar Hopscotch, heated pool and pool-deck, fitness rooms, shopping bazaar, meeting & private event spaces, business center
**Services:** Multilingual staff, room service, laundry service, pet-friendly, espresso check-in, valet parking
**Located:** Close to Marina Del Rey, Playa Vista and Los Angeles International Airport (LAX)
**Public transportation:** LAX Shuttle Service
**Map:** No. 30
**Style:** Sleek and classically modern
**What's special:** Designer hotel with open air poolside Hopscotch bar and cabanas, party room with the best view of Los Angeles International Airport, Euro minimalist style, stadium sundeck, fire pit and DJ lounge.

# The Standard Downtown

550 South Flower Street
at 6th Street
Los Angeles, CA 90071
California
Phone: +1 213 892 8080
Fax: +1 213 892 8686
www.standardhotel.com

**Price category:** $$
**Rooms:** 207 rooms
**Facilities:** Restaurant, 24 h fitness center, golf, business center, meeting rooms, rooftop pool with stunning panoramic views of LA
**Services:** Vibrating water beds, free broadband Internet service, daily maid service and dry cleaning
**Located:** Downtown Los Angeles in the financial district
**Map:** No. 31
**Style:** Contemporary design
**What's special:** Stylish downtown hotel with modern rooftop poolside bar, live DJ spins tunes twelve stories high and guests are issued bracelets to guarantee entry, and ultra-stylish rooms come in various sizes with names like Huge, Gigantic, Humongous and Wow!

# The Keating Hotel

432 F Street
San Diego, CA 92101
California
Phone: +1 619 814 5700
Fax: +1 619 814 5750
www.thekeating.com

**Price category:** $$$$
**Rooms:** 35 luxury stanzas
**Facilities:** The Vault Lounge, Minus 1 Lounge, merK restaurant and meeting space
**Services:** In-room spa, room service, personalized sip and crave bar, personalized nightly turndown service
**Located:** In San Diego's Gaslamp Quarter
**Map:** No. 32
**Style:** Modern and futuristic design
**What's special:** The Keating Hotel is the first hotel design by Pininfarina the Italian Design company behind Ferrari and Maserati; Minus 1 Lounge is the private club with vibrant red colors, stainless steel and exposed brick; 4 suites feature Pininfarina Morphosis jacuzzi tubs and the presidential suite features a private garden and outdoor jacuzzi.

KEATING

1890

# W San Diego

421 West B Street
San Diego, CA 91201
California
Phone: +1 619 398 3100
Fax: +1 619 231 5779
www.starwoodhotels.com

**Price category:** $$
**Rooms:** 258 rooms
**Facilities:** Restaurant, lounge, Beach bar, fire pit, cabanas, fitness center, spa, pool, beach
**Services:** Wireless Internet, newspaper, W hotels' dog treatment (surcharge), TV, DVD, minibar and massage are all in-room availabilities
**Located:** Three blocks from Little Italy, and five blocks from Horton Plaza and the Embarcadero
**Map:** No. 33
**Style:** Modern comfy
**What's special:** Excellent spa and fitness area, guest rooms feature Bose surround sound systems, luxury bathrooms with lemon sage products, urban rooftop beach bar on third floor.

# Korakia

257 South Patencio Road
Palm Springs, CA 92262
California
Phone: +1 760 864 6411
Fax: +1 760 864 4147
www.korakia.com

**Price category:** $$
**Rooms:** 28 unique rooms and suites
**Facilities:** Pools, library, bocce ball court, massage treatment rooms, meeting and banquet facilities
**Services:** Moroccan tea service, complimentary breakfast, WiFi access, outdoor film screenings, weekend yoga
**Located:** Center of Palm Springs, 2 h by car from LA and San Diego, 10 min to Palm Springs International Airport
**Map:** No. 34
**Style:** Moroccan and Mediterranean design
**What's special:** Two former historic artist's villas completely restored into a Greek-Moroccan designed resort of bungalows, guest houses, and heated pools set over one acre of lush gardens, lunch served poolside, hip retreat for artists, writers, and musicians.

Korakia

# Parker Palm Springs

4200 East Palm Canyon Drive
Palm Springs, CA 92264
California
Phone: +1 760 770 5000
Fax: +1 760 324 2188
www.theparkerpalmsprings.com

**Price category:** $$$$
**Rooms:** 131 rooms, 12 villas and the Gene Autry house
**Facilities:** Palm Springs Yacht Club Spa, 4 pools, tennis courts, 3 restaurants, lobby bar, indoor and outdoor firepits
**Services:** Coffee wake-up calls, 24 h room service, daily newspaper, wireless Internet access
**Located:** 10 min from downtown Palm Springs
**Public transportation:** Sun Bus
**Map:** No. 35
**Style:** Happy Luxe
**What's special:** Iconic hotel has huge comfortable rooms with hammocks on private balconies or patios, ultra-hip setting with extravagant artwork sprinkled throughout the hotel, perfectly landscaped gardens with indigenous plants and trees.

# Hope Springs

68075 Club Circle Drive
Desert Hot Springs, CA 92240
California
Phone: +1 760 329 4003
Fax: +1 760 329 4223
www.hopespringsresort.com

**Price category:** $
**Rooms:** 10 rooms
**Facilities:** 3 naturally hot mineral water fed pools, dedicated treatment room
**Services:** Complimentary continental breakfast, full menu of massages and body treatments, in-room CD player or iPod docking station
**Located:** Viewing Coachella Valley and Mount San Jacinto
**Map:** No. 36
**Style:** Relaxed minimalist modern
**What's special:** Renovated mid-century motel has only ten guest rooms with new modern minimalist interiors with Eames and Saarinen furniture, platform beds, exposed concrete floors and a groovy suspended fire-pit in the lobby, spa highlights are three mineral pools, children not allowed.

# Sagewater Spa

12689 Eliseo Road
Desert Hot Springs, CA 92240
California
Phone: +1 720 220 1554
Fax: +1 760 251 1553
www.sagewaterspa.com

**Price category:** $
**Rooms:** 7 rooms
**Facilities:** Healing mineral water pools, BBQ grill and courtyard
**Services:** Watsu pool treatment, in-room treatments like hot stone treatments, scalp reflex and thai massages, air conditioning, Internet, cable TV
**Located:** In the desert
**Map:** No. 37
**Style:** Uncluttered
**What's special:** Minimalist hotel designed with bright white and angular architecture, extensive spa treatments from aromatherapy to aloe body wraps, massive pool and 360-degree views of the mountains.

# Miracle Manor Retreat

12589 Reposo Way
Desert Hot Springs, CA 92240
California
Phone: +1 760 329 6641
US Toll Free: 877 329 6641
Fax: +1 760 329 9962
www.miraclemanor.com

**Price category:** $
**Rooms:** 6 Queen Rooms and the Cube Suite Double Twin
**Facilities:** Large soaking mineral pool, glass-enclosed hot jet spa, healing room for facials, bodywork and custom treatments
**Services:** Deluxe locally-sourced organic breakfast, customized massage packages, personalized guided nature hikes, private yoga lessons, special events packages
**Located:** 25 miles to Joshua Tree National Park
**Map:** No. 38
**Style:** Mid-Century Modern meets Zen/Contemporary
**What's special:** Desert Hot Springs spa retreat with six super-minimalist guestrooms for true urban getaway, small sanctuary is mainly focused on holistic health care with healing, hot water mineral pool and therapeutic spa treatments.

# Hotel Lucia

400 SW Broadway
Portland, OR 97205
Oregon
Phone: +1 503 225 1717
Fax: +1 503 225 1919
www.hotellucia.com

**Price category:** $$
**Rooms:** 127 rooms
**Facilities:** Typhoon! restaurant, bar, lounge, business center, meeting rooms, fitness center
**Services:** 24 h room and valet services, dry cleaning, laundry, daily maid service, minibar
**Located:** 12 miles from Portland International Airport
**Public transportation:** Max light rail
**Map:** No. 39
**Style:** Modern, minimalist, but also luxurious design
**What's special:** Design hotel focused on art and tranquil spaces, photography by Pulitzer Prize winner David Hume Kennerly hangs in the lobby and corridors, the pillow menu gives guests seven choices of pillows, including soft, firm and hypoallergenic.

800 East Burnside Street
Portland, OR 97214
Oregon
Phone: +1 503 230 9200
US Toll Free: 877 800 0004
Fax: +1 503 230 9300
www.jupiterhotel.com

**Price category:** $
**Rooms:** 80 rooms
**Facilities:** Restaurant, live entertainment nightly, Wack hair studio, Colorbomb tattoo parlor, dreamSuite, dreamBox and Think Tank creative meeting spaces
**Services:** 24 hour concierge, business services, high-speed wireless Internet, room service, spa service
**Located:** In LoBu, near Oregon Convention Center
**Map:** No. 40
**Style:** Creative Urban Boutique Hotel
**What's special:** 80-room boutique hotel with a stylish environment for the urban nomad young at heart, hip diner 21/7, popular Doug Fir bar and restaurant, cool entertainment with live bands and parties in the central courtyard.

**Art Center College Library**
**1700 Lida Street**
**Pasadena, CA 91103**

# Hotel Ändra

2000 Fourth Avenue
Seattle, WA 98121
Washington
Phone: +1 206 448 8600
Fax: +1 206 441 7140
www.hotelandra.com

**Price category:** $$$
**Rooms:** 119 rooms and suites
**Facilities:** Restaurants, full bar, fitness room and health club, meeting/banquet facilities and spa services
**Services:** 24 h concierge and room service
**Located:** In trendy Belltown
**Public transportation:** South Lake Union Trolley Car to Lake Union waterside restaurants
**Map:** No. 41
**Style:** Stylish urban hotel appealing to both the leisure traveler and the road warrior
**What's special:** Swedish-style hotel in artistic neighborhood, public spaces have a residential feel, two award-winning restaurants, guest rooms have goose down comforters, 300-thread Egyptian linens, Frette towels, and bath products by Face Stockholm.

Hotel Andra    207

# Hotel Max

620 Stewart Street
Seattle, WA 98101
Washington
Phone: +1 866 833 6299
Fax: +1 206 443 5754
www.hotelmaxseattle.com

**Price category:** $$
**Rooms:** 163 rooms
**Facilities:** The Red Fin restaurant, business center, meeting rooms
**Services:** Valet parking, high-speed wireless Internet access everywhere, 24 h room service, fitness center
**Located:** A quarter mile from Pike Place Market, 15 miles from Seattle-Tacoma International Airport
**Map:** No. 42
**Style:** Modern design
**What's special:** Stylish hotel favored by established Seattle artists and photographers, interiors have more than 350 original paintings and photographs on each floor, close proximity to first-rate shops, art galleries, fine dining and nightlife.

# Hotel Murano Tacoma

1320 Broadway Plaza
Tacoma, WA 98402
Washington
Phone: +1 253 238 8000
Fax: +1 253 591 4105
www.hotelmuranotacoma.com

**Price category:** $$
**Rooms:** 320 rooms
**Facilities:** Meeting/banquet facilities, Bite Restaurant, lobby bar, fitness center, spa and beauty services
**Services:** Flat-screen LCD televisions, VIP room services
**Located:** Next to the Tacoma convention center, 20 min to Seattle-Tacoma International Airport, 10 min to Seattle
**Public transportation:** Light rail
**Map:** No. 43
**Style:** Modern sleek design
**What's special:** Design hotel holds a world class glass art collection from over 45 artists, every guest room floor has a different theme containing the work of a single artist with photographs, artist renderings, and the glass art itself, guest rooms have luxury amenities such as in-room iPod docking station and iPod menus.

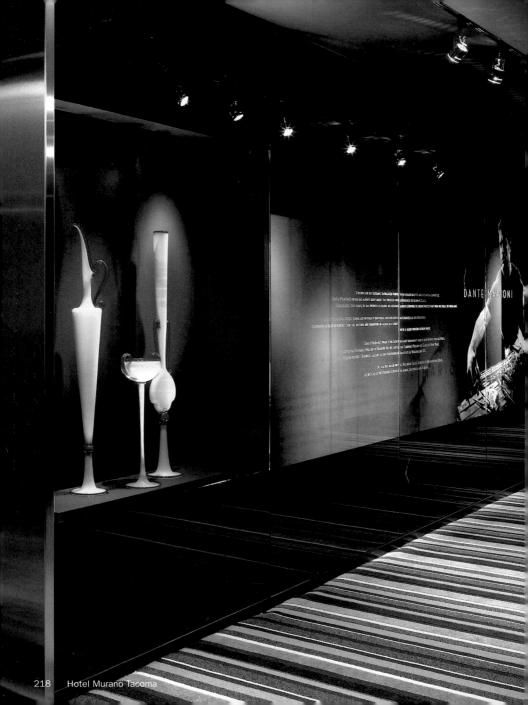